DECOD

Harcourt

SCHOOL PUBLISHERS

Copyright © by Harcourt, Inc.

Requests for permission to make copies of any part of the work should be addressed to School Permissions and Copyrights, Harcourt, Inc., 6277 Sea Harbor Drive, Orlando, Florida 32887-6777. Fax: 407-345-2418.

STORYTOWN is a trademark of Harcourt, Inc. HARCOURT and the Harcourt Logo are trademarks of Harcourt, Inc., registered in the United States of America and/or other jurisdictions.

Printed in the United States of America

ISBN 10 0-15-364118-5

ISBN 13 978-0-15-364118-3

Ordering Options
ISBN 10 0-15-364221-1
ISBN 13 978-0-15-364221-0

2 3 4 5 6 7 8 9 10   197   17 16 15 14 13 12 11 10 09 08 07

Contents

The Trade 1

Long Vowel /ā/ *a_e*

Dale Lake 9

Long Vowel /ā/ *a_e*

Mike and Spike 17

Long Vowel /ī/ *i_e*

Bikes 25

Long Vowel /ī/ *i_e*

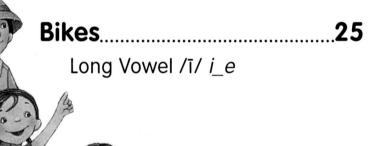

Cole and Rose Make Fake Noses **33**
Long Vowel /ō/ o_e

A Big Red Rose Grove **41**
Long Vowel /ō/ o_e

The Not-in-Tune Flute........**49**
Long Vowel /(y)o͞o/ u_e

Fun in June.............................**57**
Long Vowel /(y)o͞o/ u_e

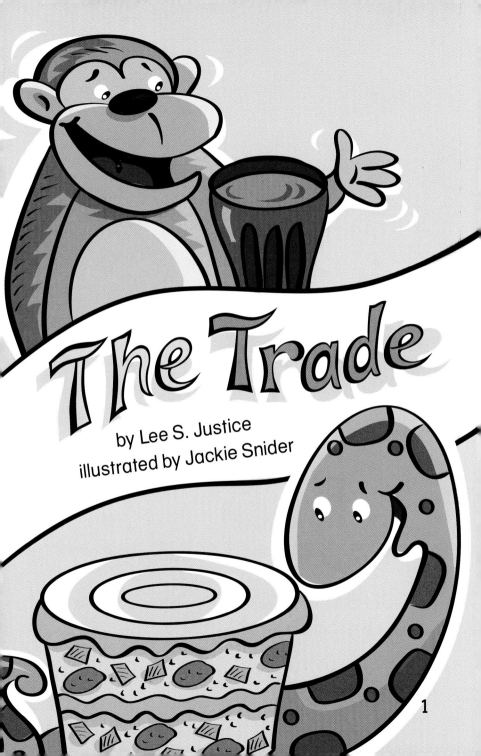

The Trade

by Lee S. Justice
illustrated by Jackie Snider

Did Snake bake a cake? Yes, Snake made a cake. It has dates and nuts in it. It is on a plate.

Did Ape make a drink? Yes, Ape made a grape drink. It is in a glass.

Snake looks at the glass. Yum! That grape drink looks good.

Ape takes a sniff of the cake on the plate. Yum! That cake smells good!

Snake gazes at Ape. Ape gazes
at Snake. They make a trade.

Will Ape save cake for Snake? Will
Snake save some drink for Ape? Yes, Ape
and Snake trade again.

Ape and Snake eat and drink together.

Dale Lake

by Laura Meredith

illustrated by Simona Mulazzani

The lane ends at a gate. It is by
a big lake. Its name is Dale Lake.

A duck sits on eggs in a safe
spot. Its mate bobs on a big wave.

Plop! What made waves? Did a
frog jump when it ate a black bug?

It is safe to swim in the lake. Wade
in. Next, take a dip and get wet.

Make up safe games. The name
of this game is Ring Toss.

It is fun to make mud cakes. Mud cakes will bake in the hot sun.

It is late. Take a last dip. Make a
date to take a trip to Dale Lake again.

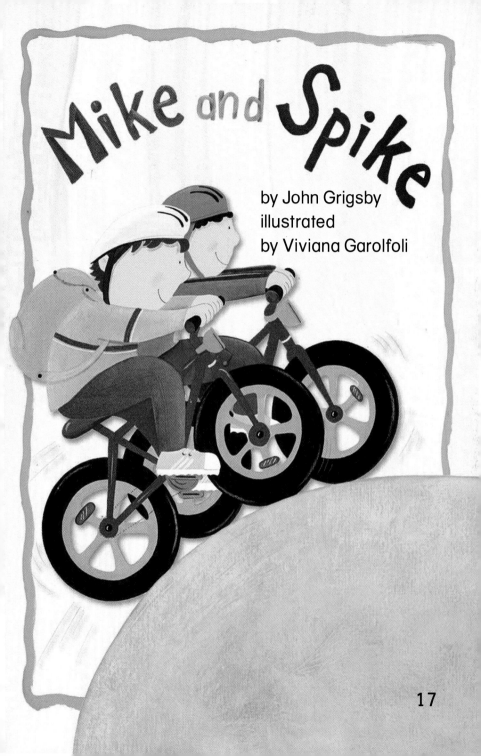

Mike and Spike

by John Grigsby
illustrated
by Viviana Garolfoli

Mike and Spike ride bikes. They ride for five miles. Mike and Spike stop at a camp site.

Mike and Spike go on a hike. Mike has a fine time. Spike does not like the hike.

Mike and Spike fly kites. One kite
rises up just fine. One kite will not rise
and dives back down.

It is time to dine on fine food. Mike bites and likes it. YUM! Spike bites and stops. YIKES!

Mike and Spike ride on a slide. Mike glides. Spike lands in a pile.

Mike and Spike ride back. Spike rides fast.

Spike rides down the drive first. He
likes to win. Now Spike can smile!

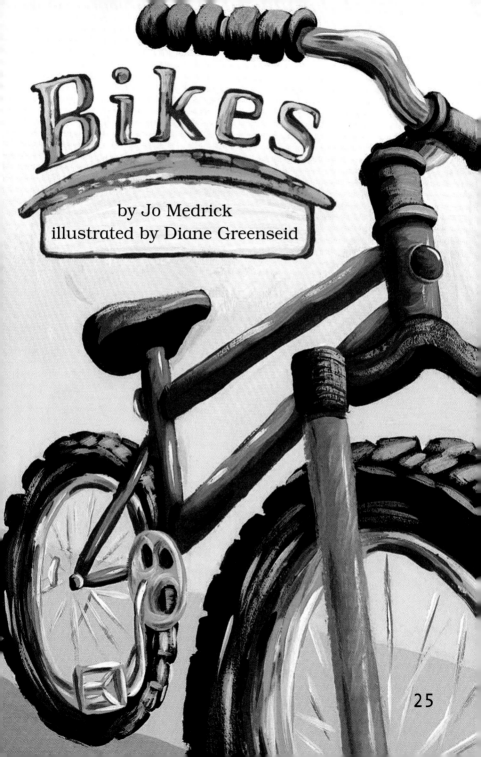

Bikes

by Jo Medrick
illustrated by Diane Greenseid

Kids like to ride bikes. Bikes are fine
to ride. Bikes make life fun.

Bikes come in lots of sizes. Little kids
ride little bikes. Big kids ride big bikes.

This bike is fine to ride up a
drive. It can ride on grass, too.

This bike is fine if you like to ride fast.
It can glide for miles and miles.

Pick a bike you like. Ike likes his red
bike. Its size is fine. Ike likes the white
stripes on its side, too.

Ike is good to his bike. Ike wipes off
grime. Ike has a lock to make it safe.

Now it is time to get on your bike and
ride off. Have a fine time!

Cole and Rose Make Fake Noses

by Ann Rossi
illustrated by Frederique Bertrand

Cole has a big fake nose. Rose likes it.

Cole makes a cone. Cole pokes two
holes in it to make a fake nose for Rose.

Cole gets string. It will hold the nose in place. Now Rose has a cone nose just like the one Cole has!

Next, Cole and Rose make a cone
nose for Bones.

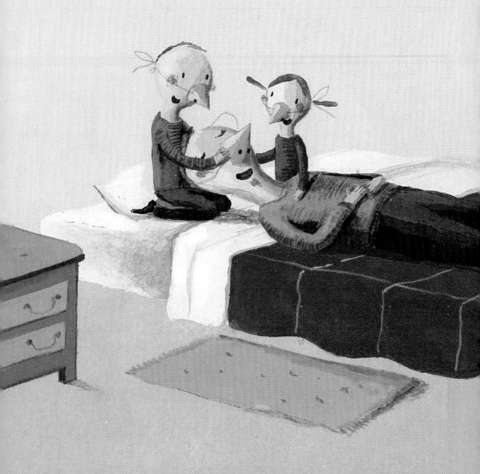

Dad dozes on his bed. Cole looks at
Dad and plans a joke. He makes a fake
nose for Dad.

Cole gets close to Dad and slips the
nose on him.

Dad wakes up. Yikes! He has a cone nose.

Dad smiles at the joke. He sees Mom.
Dad asks Cole to make a fake nose for
Mom, too.

A Big, Red Rose Grove

by Moss Stone
illustrated by Benrei Huang

Hope wants to get Mom a gift.

What can Hope get Mom?

Hope sees moles dig holes for their
homes. Hope sees hens poke holes for
bugs. Hope sees Bo dig holes for his bones.

Hope will dig holes, too. Hope will plant roses for Mom!

Hope and Dad drive and get six rose
plants. The roses have big red buds.

Hope takes the rose plants home. Hope
digs six big holes on a slope.

Hope digs up stones.

Hope sets the rose plants in the holes.

Next, Hope gets a hose and waters the roses.

Last, Hope gets Mom. What a big grove
of big red roses Mom gets from Hope! What
a big hug Hope gets from Mom!

48

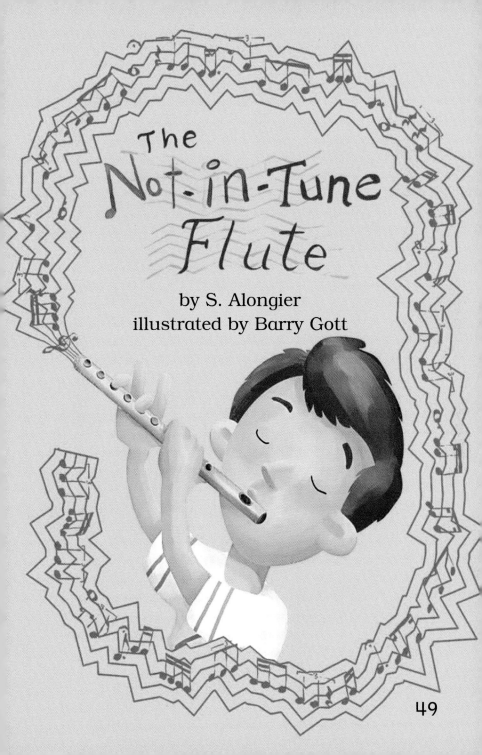

The Not-in-Tune Flute

by S. Alongier
illustrated by Barry Gott

Luke and Jude snack on some prunes.

Luke picks up his flute.

A flute is a tube that has lots of holes in it. You can use it to make tunes.

Luke makes tunes on his flute. The tunes are bad! Is his flute in tune?

Jude can not listen. Is it rude to tell
Luke to tune his flute?

Luke stops and looks in his flute. What is stuck in it? It blocks the tube.

Yuck! It is a prune. A prune is
stuck in the flute! Luke uses a stick
to get the prune.

The bad tunes were just a fluke. The flute is in tune. Luke makes a rule. Do not snack on prunes next to the flute. They can make bad tunes.

Fun in June

by Emily Bryant
Illustrated by Martha Aviles

It gets so hot in June, but you can still
have fun.

June is the best time to rest on a sand dune
and hum tunes. Use a cute hat to block the sun.

In June, skip stones on a lake. Jump in and drift on a tube! Stick to the rules and use a life vest.

You can go on a hike in June. Find a soft, white plume and use it as a fan.

June is a fine time to tune up the bike and take it on a ride. Be safe!

The June sun blazes hot in the sky. Put pop
and ice cubes in a glass and take a sip. Yum!

If you are still hot, take a ride on a flume and get wet. June is hot, but it is fun!

The Trade
Word Count: 104

High-Frequency Words	Decodable Words*	
again	a	**made**
eat	and	**make**
for	**Ape**	nuts
good	at	on
looks	**bake**	**plate**
of	**cake**	**save**
some	**dates**	smells
that	did	**Snake**
the	drink	sniff
they	**gazes**	**takes**
together	glass	**trade**
	grape	will
	has	yes
	in	yum
	is	
	it	

Boldface words indicate sound-spelling introduced in this story.

Dale Lake
Word Count: 1 13

High-Frequency Words	**Decodable Words***	
again	a	in
by	and	is
of	at	it
the	**ate**	its
this	**bake**	jump
to	big	**lake**
what	black	**lane**
	bobs	last
	bug	**late**
	cakes	**made**
	Dale	**make**
	date	**mate**
	did	much
	dip	**name**
	duck	next
	eggs	on
	ends	plop
	frog	ring
	fun	**safe**
	game	sits
	games	spot
	gate	sun
	get	swim
	hot	**take**

Boldface words indicate sound-spelling introduced in this story.

(continued)

Decodable Words*

toss
trip
up
wade
wave
waves
wet
when
will

Mike and Spike

Word Count: 114

High-Frequency Words	Decodable Words*	
does	a	**like**
down	and	**likes**
first	at	**Mike**
fly	back	**miles**
food	**bikes**	not
for	**bites**	on
go	camp	**pile**
he	can	**ride**
now	**dine**	**rides**
one	**dives**	**rise**
the	**drive**	**rises**
they	fast	**site**
to	**fine**	**slide**
	five	**smile**
	glides	**Spike**
	has	stop
	hike	stops
	in	**time**
	is	up
	it	will
	just	win
	kite	**yikes**
	kites	yum
	lands	

Boldface words indicate sound-spelling introduced in this story.

Bikes
Word Count: 120

High-Frequency Words	**Decodable Words***	
are	a	**likes**
come	and	lock
for	big	lots
good	**bike**	make
have	**bikes**	**miles**
little	can	off
now	**drive**	on
of	fast	pick
the	**fine**	red
this	fun	**ride**
to	get	safe
too	**glide**	**side**
you	grass	**size**
your	**grime**	**sizes**
	has	**stripe**
	hides	**time**
	his	up
	if	**white**
	Ike	**wipes**
	in	
	is	
	it	
	its	
	kids	
	life	
	like	

Boldface words indicate sound-spelling introduced in this story.

Cole and Rose Make Fake Noses

Word Count: 123

High-Frequency Words	**Decodable Words***	
for	a	just
he	and	like
looks	asks	likes
now	at	make
one	bed	makes
sees	big	Mom
the	**Bones**	next
to	**close**	**nose**
too	**Cole**	**noses**
two	**cone**	on
	Dad	place
	dozes	plans
	fake	**pokes**
	gets	**Rose**
	has	slips
	him	smiles
	his	string
	hold	up
	holes	wakes
	in	will
	it	yikes
	joke	

Boldface words indicate sound-spelling introduced in this story.

A Big, Red Rose Grove*
Word Count: 125

High-Frequency Words	Decodable Words	
for	a	**hose**
from	and	hug
have	big	in
of	Bo	last
sees	**bones**	**moles**
the	buds	Mom
their	bugs	next
to	can	on
too	Dad	plant
wants	dig	plants
waters	digs	**poke**
what	drive	red
	get	**rose**
	gets	**roses**
	gift	sets
	grove	six
	hens	**slope**
	his	**stones**
	holes	takes
	home	up
	homes	will
	Hope	

Boldface words indicate sound-spelling introduced in this story.

The Not-in-Tune Flute*
Word Count: 138

High-Frequency Words	Decodable Words	
are	a	next
do	and	not
listen	bad	on
looks	blocks	picks
of	can	**prune**
some	**fluke**	**prunes**
that	**flute**	**rude**
the	get	**rule**
they	has	snack
to	his	stick
what	holes	stops
were	in	stuck
you	is	tell
	it	**tube**
	Jude	**tune**
	just	**tunes**
	lots	up
	Luke	**use**
	make	**uses**
	makes	yuck

*Boldface words indicate sound-spelling introduced in this story.

Fun in June
Word Count: 142

High-Frequency Words	Decodable Words*	
are	a	ice
have	and	if
put	as	in
sky	be	is
the	best	it
to	bike	jump
you	blazes	**June**
	block	lake
	but	life
	can	on
	cubes	**plume**
	cute	pop
	drift	rest
	dune	ride
	fan	**rules**
	find	safe
	fine	sand
	flume	sip
	fun	skip
	get	so
	gets	soft
	glass	stick
	go	still
	hat	stones
	hike	sun
	hot	take

Boldface words indicate sound-spelling introduced in this story.

(continued)

Decodable Words*

time

tube

tune

tunes

up

use

vest

wet

white

yum

*Boldface words indicate sound-spelling introduced in this story.